AUTHOR-IZE

The Speed Authoring System to Grow Your Business FAST

How to Quickly Position Yourself as The Authority, Build Your Brand, Attract Quality Leads, and Increase Your Income

CYDNEY O'SULLIVAN

AUTHOR-IZE

The Speed Authoring System to Grow Your Business FAST

For general information on our other products and services, please find our contact information online at **www.CelebrityExperts.com**

Special thank you to Dr Dion Klein for cover photo

Designed and Published By
Celebrity Publishing LLC
Las Vegas, Nevada, USA +1 702 997 2229
Sydney, Australia +61 2 8005 4878
www.CelebrityPublishers.com

Thank you for investing in

AUTHOR-IZE

The Speed Authoring System to Grow Your Business FAST

How To Position Yourself As An Authority, Attract Quality Leads, Increase Your Income and Build Your Brand ... Effortlessly

Join and receive bonus resources and tools worth over $1,200!

www.CelebrityExperts.com/book-bonuses

Join our email community and each month you'll receive surprise bonuses from the author and contributors worth over $1,200 in value! Please visit the website for more information

Join our free author community on Facebook, you'll be regularly invited to our trainings and tips for authors. I hope you'll join us over at

https://www.facebook.com/groups/celebrityexperts/

ABOUT THE AUTHOR

Cydney O'Sullivan

Best-Selling Author • Entrepreneur • International Speaker Branding & Publishing Consultant

You've probably heard that writing a book that showcases your business or expertise is one of the most impactful things you can ever do. More than a book, you create a powerful marketing and authority positioning tool.

The process of writing and planning a book will give clarity to your marketing message, reinforce your expertise and establish your authority.

Cydney O'Sullivan is a multiple best-selling author, award-winning international speaker and communications consultant who helps experts and businesses stand out from their competitors.

Cydney draws on decades of experience in her role as an author, publisher, speaker, and marketing consultant to share insider secrets learned over decades working with successful experts to create your '**Magnificent Million Dollar Message.**'

She helps experts to boost your reach and bottom line through strategic social media marketing. As a recognized influencer, her business advice has been featured in national newspapers and magazines and in many best-selling books.

She was listed as one of the **top 10 Motivational Speakers in Australia** and in the best-selling books **The World's Greatest Speakers, Motivational Speakers Australia and Motivational Speakers America** with highly esteemed celebrities such as Brian Tracy, Les Brown, Allan Pease and Suze Orman.

After building businesses for over 30 years, Cydney believes that thanks to modern technologies one of the fastest and most cost-effective ways to create wealth today is **building your authority and personal earning power through Celebranding™ – a system she designed to build your personal brand with celebrity leverage**.

"Social media is bigger, more important and far more influential than any television channel or internet website. But here comes the good Ms O'Sullivan proving that used properly, social media can make a fortune for you far more rapidly than TV or email. It need not explode in your face before it causes a profit explosion in your bank account…"

—*Jay Conrad Levinson, The Father of Guerrilla Marketing,*
  over 21 million books sold

From multi-millionaires to cutting-edge resource providers who are creating tools to make social marketing fast, fun and easy, Cydney has gathered insights that will make a difference to the bottom-line of any business.

—*Dr Daryl Grant, Internet Marketing Consultant*

Find out more at **www.CelebrityExperts.com**

TABLE OF CONTENTS

BONUS CHAPTER 4

INTRODUCTION

How to quickly write your book series and then turn all that content into an automated authority marketing and money making system

There are a lot of reasons to write a book but most critically, when done right, your book will become one of your business and personal brand's most potent positioning and marketing tools.

For almost two decades now I've worked as a marketing consultant to entrepreneurs in a multitude of industries and niches, helping them to clarify and communicate their personal brands and become best-selling authors.

I look for ways to add extra personal revenue streams through presentations, webinars, training programs and consulting. Over the last few years, I have become a book mentor for business coaching communities, and I now help hundreds of people each year to write, publish and promote their books.

But I never start with the book. I begin by defining the long-term goals and aspirations of the authors and what they are building. Their book, you see, is a foundational step in launching a celebrity identity for the author that, with focus and determination, can easily be leveraged into a powerful celebrity brand. Are you feeling excited and a little nervous?

Why I Wrote This Book

This book has been written to answer the questions that I get repeatedly asked by people wanting to know how to live their dreams, create their legacy, increase their income and help more people.

Perhaps there's a topic of expertise that you are repeatedly asked about? What are the questions that you're asked over and over again? Maybe you could write a book about them? Wouldn't that save you a lot of time?

One of my clients recorded some of her initial client meetings and simply turned all those questions and answers into a book series that she now requires her clients to purchase and read before they start working together. This has allowed her to free up so much of her time that she was able to take on twice as many clients, and raise her prices. Could that work for you?

I love working with coaches, consultants, professionals and experts to help them produce professional books and then expand them into automated online and live training programs. Many professionals are paid for the limited time they have available. The trick is to set up systems that allow you to sell your experience over and over.

Doing this is so much more scaleable – there are literally no limits to how many copies of your book you can get out into the world. Once it's out there, you can start making a difference for others as well as bringing in more qualified prospects and leads for your business.

The reason I am so passionate about this topic is that two years ago I survived cancer but not before going through five surgeries and nine months of treatments. As you can probably imagine, the most I could do at this time was to work part-time. But because my business relied so heavily on me working, I lost that business and hundreds of thousands of dollars that I had put into building it.

What I have learned is that life or market conditions can change at any time with little or no notice. So, the more you can automate your business, the more freedom that gives you, and the more you can work ON instead of IN your business.

Case Study: Your Million Dollar Message book

I have written quite a few books over the years, and each of them I've used to market a coaching program.

Here's an example of one that has worked very successfully.

I wrote an eBook called Your Million Dollar Message, How to Be a Highly Paid Speaker, Trainer or Consultant. This fitted with my work because I was helping speakers to improve their marketing as well as running a lot of events. My ideal clients, therefore, were speakers, trainers and consultants.

I promoted the eBook as part of a free gift campaign to speakers' groups and had hundreds of speakers and trainers apply to find out more about getting our help with their marketing.

We had so many applications that we saw a gap in the market and launched a boutique marketing agency with several hundred clients.

I estimate that the revenues this book has indirectly generated to date are well over half a million dollars.

If you'd like to get a copy of that book go grab a copy of Your Million Dollar Message eBook at **https://celebrityexperts.com/mdmbook**

After losing my business, I found I was in demand for my expertise in book marketing. Since then, I have helped hundreds of experts become best-selling published authors. And now, it's your turn!

I regularly work with experts who use their books to attract thousands of highly targeted leads and buyers to their business and generate hundreds of thousands of dollars in scaleable revenues.

How to Create Your 'Million Dollar Message'

You certainly don't need to publish a book to be successful, but you will undoubtedly benefit from the process. If you follow the system I outline for you here, the right book can be a huge asset to your marketing. This applies to anyone with an interest in writing a book that helps others, or who already has written a book (or books) that they know could be used more effectively.

Perhaps you've already written a book, but you feel that it doesn't fit this system? Or maybe it doesn't fit with your message to the world anymore?

The good news is that you can easily write another one once you see how powerful getting your message right actually is. In fact, today, more than ever, creating a clear 'Power Message' and promoting it to your ideal target market so that they understand who YOU ARE and WHO you help, and HOW, is absolutely critical. Even more so as we get bombarded with information, advertising and our businesses compete on a global level.

If the idea of becoming a 'Celebrity Expert' scares you a little bit, and you wonder if you're ready to put your life in the 'spotlight' for all to judge, that's a good thing. It means you're like most of the experts I've worked with, who begin this process wondering if they're smart enough / good enough / educated enough.

It's a very natural and understandable concern which is why the system I'm outlining helps you grow into your public persona one logical and supported step at a time.

I believe it starts with some soul searching to find your own personal mission, vision and reason. These things will carry you through all the challenges and doubts along the way. Writing a book requires discipline which in turn, helps you hone in your message. I regularly witness the transformation that writing a book does to people's lives.

You can also use this system to write your memoirs, fiction, novels or other types of books. However, I want to keep things simple, so have focused on how to write books for lead collection and client attraction purposes.

Most people are put off writing a book because they think it will take weeks, months or years, but with this system, you can write your book in a few hours or a few days.

Why Write a Book?

Writing and publishing a professional book:

❯ Establishes your expertise and authority

❯ Gives you much greater credibility

❯ Introduces you to prospects

❯ Allows you to easily share information

❯ Makes you more attractive as a speaker, media interview and an expert in your field

❯ Allows you to share your ideas and expertise with people who might not ordinarily know of you or be able to afford you

Which do you think a prospect will hold onto for longer – your business card, brochure or your book? Now, thanks to digital delivery, we don't even have to provide a physical book –fortunes are being made from PDF books just like this one.

Why It's Hard For Most People to Write A Book

Do you read books? Would you find it difficult to write one yourself? It's my experience that so many professionals know they SHOULD write a book, or WANT to write one, but are so overwhelmed for one reason or another that it never gets done.

That's why I'm excited to share this simple system with you to help you write a book that you can be proud of in as little as two days.

In my 7 Steps to Write Your Book Fast, you'll be able to produce your first book and then, if you choose to, repeat the process over and over. When you witness the power a book harnesses as a marketing tool through the examples shared in this book, you'll be raring to go!

The 7 Step Speed System to Write Your Book FAST!

Step 1: Plan Your Book

Step 2: Choose your chapter points and stories

Step 3: Storyboard Your Book

Step 4: Dictate or write your book

Step 5: Edit & Review Your Book

Step 6: Format Your Book & Cover

Step 7: Share Your Book

The best news having written your book, you will have a store of organized information that you can repurpose to create valuable client attraction systems such as:

❯ Presentations

❯ Training programs

❯ Webcasts

❯ Powerful marketing campaigns that can be automated and turned into ongoing client attraction systems.

What if Someone Else Can Write Your Book, Presentations, Training Programs and Marketing for you?

This may come as a surprise but writing your book yourself might not be the best use of your time and talents. Thought-leaders over generations have dictated their insights and ideas to talented scribes.

In fact, many professional non-fiction books are written by professional writers with guidance from the author. This is known as hiring a ghost-writer.

You may be surprised to learn that these books were written by ghost-writers:

❯ Richard Branson in Losing My Virginity, acknowledging Edward Whitley

❯ Michael Crichton in Latitudes (finished posthumously)

❯ Alexandre Dumas in The Three Musketeers and The Count of Monte Cristo

❯ Ian Fleming, creator of James Bond

❯ Hilary Clinton in Living History, acknowledging Maryanne Vollers

❯ Jack Welch in Jack: Straight From the Gut, "with John Byrne"

❯ Jack Welch also writes books with his wife Suzy Welch, former Editor-In-Chief of the Harvard Business Review

❯ Stephen Covey in The 7 Habits of Highly Effective People with Ken Shelton

❯ Donald Trump in The Art of the Deal, "with Tony Schwartz"

❯ Tom Clancy, Robert Ludlum and James Patterson

Even if you end up choosing to hire one of our ghost-writers to write your book, or to get book coaching, you'll still need to flesh out the structure and main messages for the book. That's why I'm going to give you my step-by-step system to plan out your book and get it written FAST.

Have you noticed how many top marketers have written books despite knowing how to market in plenty of other ways? That's because it's been repeatedly proven that having a book that addresses the specific problems of your ideal clients can dramatically reduce your marketing costs, shorten your buying cycle and help to raise your fees.

Many marketers use an eBook as an authority building 'lead magnet' to give away either for free or at low cost, in exchange for contact information. If your book provides a solution to a problem, there's a good chance that the people who want your book are looking for **that** solution.

Example: <u>CelebrityExperts.com</u>

We help experts and authorities to become 'celebrity experts' in their field. We do this by helping them to write a book, create a program to sell beyond the book, and set up their marketing systems for ongoing success.

If you are reading this book, you're probably interested in learning how we do this, and how we can do it for you. I have written this guide in step-by-step format, so you can achieve your result faster and with confidence, and to build a relationship with you by providing genuine solutions.

I encourage you to write your client attraction book with this same purpose. To do so, I will share some inspiring examples, and talk you through book marketing campaigns that can generate tens of thousands to millions of dollars in revenue.

Statistics show that about 80%+ of people with a story to tell and an education (the majority of people surveyed) say they would like to write a book. But, even though it's easier today than ever before, only a tiny percentage of these people actually write their book and get it published.

At the time of writing, there are around 7.5 billion people on our planet, and about 326 million are in the USA. According to surveys and poll results quoted on the web, 81% of Americans (approximately 260 million of them) say they believe they have a book 'in them' that they should write and publish. However, less than a million new titles are released around the world each year according to **http://www.worldometers. info/books/**.

Experts on the topic speculate that about 90% of the people who do start a book never complete and publish them. My goal is to help you to be one of the elite few who do achieve your goals.

I know of lots of reasons why people DON'T write their books. As a creative person I find it easy to come up with ideas for books and businesses, but seeing ideas through to completion can be challenging. Sensitive and creative people can find it confronting to present their innovations or creations. We worry that people will judge our product or service and find fault, or worse – find **us** less than brilliant?

Another reason that people don't start or finish their books? They want them to be unique, or perfect, or extraordinary. Others simply feel too busy to write. However, I think the majority I meet could easily write a book, they just don't know how to pull it all together.

That's how I felt when I finally committed to finishing some of the projects I'd started. I spent a fortune hiring ghostwriters, editors, and mentors to help me, but it just confused me more – there was so much to write about, how would I pack it into a single book?

I started doing training programs on how to write best-selling books, how to get in the media, how to create presentations, webinars, training programs... I became a perpetual student, overcoming my own self-sabotage and writing books in my own name as well as hundreds as a ghostwriter and publisher for other experts.

I teach my clients how to write and promote their books through my training program at Celebrity Blueprint

8 Online Trainings

- Lesson 1- Discover your Million Dollar Message
- Lesson 2- How to write your bestselling book
- Lesson 3- How to publish and promote your bestselling book
- Lesson 4- How to create your persuasive Million Dollar Message presentation
- Lesson 5- How to get your book featured in US and Australian media
- Lesson 6- How to set up your Automation Sequence
- Lesson 7- How to create your own events and profit
- Lesson 8- How to attract leads to your business

($1000 value)

Plus these bonus trainings:

- Lesson 1 – Tips For Writing Your Best Selling Book
- Lesson 2 – The Psychology of Brands
- Lesson 3 – Using Guerrilla Publicity To Promote Your Book
- Lesson 4 – Securing Corporate Sponsors
- Lesson 5 – Getting Celebrity Endorsements & TV Exposure
- Lesson 6 – Planning A Successful Promotion
- Lesson 7 – Get That Book Written In 5 Days!!
- Lesson 8 – Create Audio Products To Make Money While You Write Your Book
- Lesson 9 – Dummies Book Literary Agent Interview
- Lesson 10 – Interview with a Hay House Publisher's Agent
- Lesson 11 – Successful Author Steve Olsher Interview
- Lesson 12 – Successful Author Michael Maher Interview
- Lesson 13 – Set Up A Content Creation Machine
- Lesson 14 – Get More Clients, More Fun, and More Money!

($1997 value)

The good news is that you don't have to go through the thousands of hours that I did to learn what works, and what doesn't. In Write A Book In A Day, I'm going to break it down into a step-by-step system, explaining the complex aspects of the process as well as going into more depth.

This system has helped hundreds of people to write, publish and market their books including cookbooks, poetry books, biographies, and children's books, so be assured it can work for you. For the purposes of this book we are going to focus on how to plan and write a great business book, and use it to promote and grow your business.

When planning a book to promote your business it's worth pointing out that you can use this book to be in the public eye for a long time, so we'll spend time on how to build a 'brand' and choose the topics of expertise that you will enjoy teaching, consulting about and talking about for many years.

Your book will allow you to be in your greatest flow, to grow and evolve and build a personal legacy that you can take with you from job to job, company to company, and will last longer than your own lifetime.

The STARS System

There is a proven system that experts have used in one form or another for decades to build their celebrity brand. The internet has made it possible to do it much faster and made it more affordable than ever before. After working with hundreds of experts as a marketing consultant to add more revenue to their business, I created a system to teach my clients how to build their celebrity brands.

I call it the STARS system. It's as an easy way to explain the foundational steps to building up a strong, income-generating brand in the most effective way.

The STARS Success System

S – **Start with your Strengths** – focus on a topic of expertise that is a natural fit for you

T – **Target Your Tribe** – spend time really getting clear on who is your ideal community, from customers to support network and mentors

A – **Authority** – start writing and promoting your books, trainings, videos and being on social media and traditional media – to build up your authority and thought leadership status

R – **Revenue** – focus on your monetization models and expand your reach with more advanced marketing strategies

S – **Scale** – what's working that you can now do more of? Start adding more leverage, growth and more streams of income and influence.

I have seen this system work over and over for the people who follow it. You don't have to be a genius, or exceptional. Just apply consistent focus.

You'll learn how to attract dozens of your ideal clients into your business and how you can scale your business exponentially by adding thousands of targeted prospects to your mailing list by adding marketing and advertising (see our forthcoming guides).

Frequently Asked Questions
(Popular topics on book coaching calls)

1. **How many pages should my book be?**

    The popular length for an authority book is currently around 100 pages, this looks like a fast book to read, while still feeling like a full book.

2. **How many words should the book contain?**

    It depends on your book size, font size and page layout. We generally advise our clients to write books with about 30,000 to 50,000 words.

3. **I have so many ideas or areas of expertise, which book should I write?**

    What are your long-term, short-term and mid-term goals? Take some time to think about which book topic is going to help you achieve your most important goals over the short, medium and long term.

4. **What size should my book be?**

    For Digital books, for the US market, use Letter Size (8.5"x11"), for the Australian and European markets use A4 (210mm x 297mm).

    Printed books the most popular size is 6"x9" because of optimal printing conditions, common variations are 5"x8" for more of a 'pocket sized' book, or 7"x10" for something bigger that stands out on the bookshelf.

5. **How much will it cost to print my books**

    The answer is… it depends. How long is a piece of string? If you want to keep your print costs down keep your page count low (the more pages, the more printing, the heavier the book and the more it will cost to print and ship), the size of your book standard (6"x9"), and print in greyscale or black and white.

If you want to print in small quantities, you'll probably pay a premium for that in printing and shipping costs. Adding color to your printing will add to your print costs, some printers will let you choose the thickness of your paper and covers. For instance you may want to use bulky but lightweight paper to make your book feel more substantial.

I can tell you that generally one 6"x9" book of around 100 pages with black and white on white paper interiors currently costs about $2.50 plus shipping to print wholesale from Amazon's publishing platform **KDP.com**. But the shipping costs might surprise you, depending where you need the books delivered to.

Since Print on Demand technology has disrupted the printing industry it pays to shop around or have a good relationship with a printer.

The rule of thumb is that with larger print runs the cost per book gets lower as the bulk of the cost is in the initial print run setup. But this generally means printing thousands of copies to get significant discounts.

Printing costs can also vary from printer to printer, and country to country.

6.   **How do you get your authors Best Seller Status?**

We promote our book launches through thousands of emails, submissions to multiple book promotion sites, tens of thousands of social media followers and book readers.

We can also run media campaigns, ad campaigns, pre-launch campaigns, free giveaways. We're always looking for ways to promote our clients books!

7. **How do other publishers promote books?**

    Many publishers don't promote their books anymore, so it's important to find out before you sign with a publisher if that is included, how they'll be promoting and if it's going to cost you extra.

    I have clients who have invested tens to hundreds of thousands of dollars with their publisher or PR agents on promotions services for their books. This makes sense if you have a strategic marketing plan and an effective ROI strategy in place. But unfortunately most authors don't.

    As a boutique publisher, we focus on working with a limited number of authors and offer promotion solutions to match our client's goals, for budgets from $500 to $500,000.

8. **How do I make money with my books?**

    When you've read this book you'll see that I've given you a LOT of ways that your book can quickly be turned into extra income.

    It can be as simple as selling your books anywhere there's a crowd that might like your book (and they'll let you sell it!)... to using your book as part of exciting and complex marketing campaigns.

The good news is that when you join our free author community on Facebook, you'll be regularly invited to our trainings and tips for authors.

I hope you'll join us over at

https://www.facebook.com/groups/celebrityexperts/

And remember at **Celebrity Experts** we'd love to help you write, publish and promote your book!

We also teach our authors how to run great webinars, prepare power presentations, and set up online training programs! So come join our community!

Now are you ready to 'power plan' out your book?

Creative people can have trouble choosing one of the many ideas they have for a book or training program. Remember, there are no right or wrong answers, I believe you have lots of books to write!

So for speed to market I suggest tapping into the knowledge, experience, expertise and any trainings, articles, blog posts, presentation scripts and programs that you already have.

CHAPTER 1
STEP 1: Plan Your Book

What's Your Main Goal For The Book?

> To attract qualified and interested prospects to your business?

> To tell your compelling story?

> To teach something valuable that your target market wants/needs to know?

The main goals for My Book are:

_____

_____

_____

_____

_____

_____

_____

_____

It's important to be clear and identify your primary goal(s) for your book so that you create a book that achieves these.

Now choose the type of book you want to write:

1. **A 'How-To' Instructions Book**

2. **___ Ways to _____ book (e.g. 50 ways to Market Your Business)**

3. **Collection of Stories Book (e.g. Inspirational stories or Top Tips from Experts)**

4. **Overcoming a Challenge book (Recall or set a challenge and tell your story)**

5. **Your memoir or biography**

6. **A 'Mistakes to avoid' book**

Case Study:
SOCIAL MARKETING SUPERSTARS Book

This is an example of learning the hard way after landing a publishing contract from a major publisher. The publisher approved my proposal to write a book called the Fast Millionaire Formula. I set about interviewing some of the most successful business strategists I knew to obtain their advice on how to make millions while building a socially supportive and conscious business.

This type of book is brilliant for aligning yourself with highly esteemed celebrity experts, and for becoming more of an expert through the process of research, interviewing and writing the book.

This type of book does take a lot longer to piece together as you must set up the interviews, (or get the contributors to write their own chapters), transcribe, collate, get their approval, etc. It's a major project.

Looking back at Social Marketing Superstars, I developed long-term relationships with many of the experts I interviewed for the book, and have since partnered with them on a number of projects.

At the time I was known for making millions in business, real estate and share investing and I wanted to help more people by becoming an author and information marketer. The Fast Millionaire Formula book would have been in line with my positioning and business goals.

However, the publishers decided that the book sounded too "get rich quick" and insisted that I choose another name for the book.

Because the underlying theme of the book was the social marketing aspect I changed it to Social Marketing Superstars, and although the book became a best seller, it didn't naturally lead customers to my business, so I found it harder to use effectively for attracting my ideal clients.

With this the **Author-ize Fast Authoring** system I find it's easier to write new books than to rewrite old ones. That's why I'm writing books and creating training programs that specifically address the issues that I see delay my clients from achieving the greater success and automation they dream of and deserve.

I recently outlined my entire system to help clients become 'Celebrity Experts' in their industry, and I have found it to be so helpful in planning out all our marketing moving forward.

I now have my entire system neatly mapped out and organized, which means we can create books, trainings, live workshops, articles, blog posts, podcasts and so on. The clarity of my expertise has attracted a lot of high -level new business opportunities.

Here are some questions to help you plan and name your books:

1. WHO do you want to attract with your book?

_____

_____

_____

_____

2. Who are your ideal clients?

_____

_____

_____

_____

3. What are the problems you solve for them?

_____

_____

_____

_____

4.   Why are you writing this book?

_____

_____

_____

_____

5.   Who will it appeal to?

_____

_____

_____

_____

6.   Will it inspire your target prospects to want to work with you?

_____

_____

_____

_____

For example, your book can help you create more income through:

1.   Book tours or taking booths at events or marketplaces and selling copies of your books (ideally bundled with a coaching program that brings the value and price up!)

2.   Being paid as a speaker or trainer on your topic of expertise

3.   Bringing leads to your business

4.   Expanding it into training, coaching or consulting programs.

5.   Expanding it into a book series, regular workshops, webcasts or podcasts

Whichever you choose, remember to market it along with your book.

If you have already written an eBook, could you expand it into a full book of about 30,000 to 50,000 words, around 80 -100 pages long?

> **Spoiler alert: If you've half written or already written a book, and it's not the right book – one that attracts your ideal clients – it might be easier to start afresh.**

Defining Your Avatar:
Who Is Your Ideal Customer?

In this book, I refer to your IDEAL CLIENT – because to have a successful client attraction book, you need to know who those best clients are. Doing so means you can talk to them in their language and address their unique problems.

If you want to sell anything, it's important that you don't make the common mistake of believing that you understand everybody and know what they all want and need.

When businesses start out this way, they lack focus and are effectively heading blindfold into the world without knowing who their potential customer is or what they need. You know what they say: If you attempt to attract everyone – your business will attract no one.

To find your target tribe you need to understand them inside and out. That's where avatars come in. Why do entrepreneurs love using the word 'avatar' when discussing their ideal customer? Because an avatar can help your business succeed and grow.

Your avatar will represent the customer who is looking for the wonderfully unique, helpful and reliable information that your business offers. Your business will be solving this customer's agony point(s) and offering exactly what they need. It's because of customers like your avatar that you will thrive rather than dwindle.

Think of this book as the first of many that you will write and publish. Focus on this as number one in a series of many and keep it simple.

What is your Book's Main Message?

1. Who are the clearly defined target audience you are writing this book for (be as specific as possible)?

_____

_____

_____

_____

_____

_____

2. Where does your target audience connect? How can you reach them? Facebook, Linkedin, an association, networking groups, etc.?

_____

_____

_____

_____

_____

_____

_____

3. If your target audience could tell you their problems. What would they be?

_____

_____

_____

_____

_____

4. Of the problems listed above, which of these solutions can your book solve?

_____

_____

_____

_____

_____

_____

Choosing Your Final Book Title and Sub Title

To plan your book, it helps to start with a 'working title.' I find it's easier to come up with a final title and subtitle once the book has been written. You can market test different titles and find the best one by split-testing campaigns, engaging with your clients and peers and getting your community on board during the pre-launch of your book.

Title and Subtitle Rule of thumb:

Your title should be short, clear and memorable. Your subtitle should explain the result or benefit a reader will get from your book.

So right now, try brain dumping some working titles and subtitles for your book and book series:

Working Titles:

_____

_____

_____

_____

_____

_____

_____

Subtitles:

_____

_____

_____

_____

_____

_____

_____

_____

Recap: Take a Few Moments To Answer These Questions:

1. What is the main result you want to achieve with this book?

   _____

2. Who is the audience you want to reach with this book?

   _____

3. What topics do you know to be of interest to this audience?

   _____

4. What would be valuable information to this audience?

   _____

5. Do you have any articles, blog posts or presentation scripts already written on these topics you can use to help write your book faster?

   _____

6. Do you have any books already on your topic to give you inspiration for structure and content?

_____

7. Is it worth going to the bookstore or library to get some?

_____

How to Research Your Book Topic and Title

Once you've got some ideas for books that would enhance and showcase your existing business. It's worth doing some research to see what others in your area of expertise are writing about and get ideas for your book title, because coming up with the right title and subtitle for your book is really important.

Shortlist your possible book titles to a list of 3-5 books you'd like to produce. Then type your topic into the Google search bar and see what's coming up on the first few pages of Google for that topic.

What you're looking for is how popular is this topic, are there forums where you can go in and see what problems people are saying they have on this topic? Does it look like there's plenty of demand?

If it's a really popular topic, look for your own unique angle. How to write a book is a really popular topic, and lots of people have written books about it, but you ended up with my book, didn't you? And it's possible that you've read other books and bought training programs on how to write a book, and may do so again.

I won't try to pack keyword analysis training into this book, but if you know how to do in-depth keyword analysis, and build high demand search terms into your book name and description, it can help your book and trainings show up more places online, especially if you opti-mize your webpages and relevant marketing.

Some sites you can use for that are:

❯ Google Adwords Keyword Planner,

❯ there's a great free tool *at* https://neilpatel.com/ubersuggest/,

❯ and some advanced tools at https://www.wordstream.com/key-words,

❯ https://keywordtool.io

❯ https://buzzsumo.com

Other places to research your topic are book sites such as Amazon.com, Goodreads.com, Bookdepository.com. and sites where people sell their courses. (Some of these might be a fit to sell your courses later).

❯ https://www.lynda.com/

❯ https://www.udemy.com/

❯ https://www.udacity.com/

❯ https://www.skillshare.com/

My advice for coming up with your final book name is to do a free flow brain dump of every possible combination of names you can think of for about 15 minutes. Type or write out about 30 – 40 possible names, and try to pack as much inviting information into the title and subtitle about the book as you can in as few words as possible.

Sometimes if you scan through your book after you've written it, you'll find that a sentence or heading in your book pops out as being a great name for your book. That was how I came up with the subtitle **Social Media Mystery to Mastery in 30 Days** for my book **Social Marketing Superstars**.

CHAPTER 2

STEP 2: Choose Your Chapter Points and Stories

Remember a client attraction book's purpose is to provide exceptional value *and* solve a problem for your target market. Your book should, therefore, be full of genuine value and not a sales brochure for your business.

Although we're all living with information overload, we're lucky to be in business at a time in history where the need for organized information is in very high demand.

So, congratulations on all the expertise you've accumulated to date in your life. Right now, there are so many people turning to experts for so many different areas of their life whether it be related to their health, wealth, relationships, or you name it.

Remember, there's currently a huge demand for your expertise; as a coach, counsellor, consultant, trainer or educator.

If you're like me, you will have spent a small fortune on training, on mentors and programs to teach you more. Some of it has probably worked, and some of it was a complete waste of your time and money. Perhaps it wasn't the right fit, or you weren't ready for it?

Maybe you invested thousands in college and finished up with a degree that you were no longer passionate about? I know of people who've racked up $100,000 + in personal debt, which will take them years to pay off. I'm here to show you a better way.

I'm sure you already know that packaging up your expertise can be a big money business. I've invested in several mentors and mentoring programs. I have mentors right now to improve different aspects of my life as well as my business where I've literally spent hundreds of thousands, but the ROI was easily worth it because I've turned their mentoring into multiple millions in my lifetime.

Why Have 'A Million Dollar Message?'

You already know you've got a great product, have excellent sales people on board (including yourself), and your social media is up and running so why do you need a message?

Simply put, your message is the quickest way to communicate with and connect with your target audience/ideal customer. These are, after all, the very same people who are looking for you and your product to solve their agony points.

What would happen if each time you make an appearance, your message alters? You'll appear as if you don't know where you're coming from and your target audience will be confused.

Getting Your Million Dollar Message Down on Paper

When it comes to creating your million-dollar message, now is not the time to be wishy-washy. You need to convey to your target audience exactly 'what' makes you different to your competitors, 'why' you are the right fit for them, and to top it off, you need to do so memorably. Often, using your own experiences within your message can add impact and help the customer relate to you on a personal level.

To start developing your million-dollar message begin by asking:

1. What is the business/product/service I am offering?

2. Why have I created this business/product/service?

3. What agony points does my company/business/product solve or seek to help the customer with?

Perfecting your Message

There's no doubt that your message will take time to perfect, especially as it will need to be adjusted over time. Therefore, don't wait for it to be 100% perfect before you go out there and share or you'll never get beyond it being on paper. Realistically, you will need to tweak your message as your business progresses. Consider it as organic – tend to it over time and be prepared to prune, tether and grow…

At Celebrity Experts, one of the first problems we help clients with is realizing the value of their lifetime's experience. After all, if we don't fully believe in ourselves, we'll never be able to command top dollar. And if we don't understand how valuable our expertise is, we have no idea how much more we could be charging or why others would want to pay more.

To achieve higher fees and credible expert status among peers, there are a few shortcuts that will make a huge difference in your business. Writing a book is one of these, in fact, it's **THE** most powerful fast-track authority and positioning tool.

Remember, your Book can be Brilliant for your Business

❯ To establish your authority

❯ As a lead magnet or conversation starter

❯ To create email nurturing sequences

❯ As the basis for a training program

❯ To promote you as a speaker

❯ To promote yourself as a consultant or elite in your field

Experience has shown me that the biggest challenge us experts face is that we don't stand out in our marketplace and, that we don't spend enough time focusing on the problems we solve.

Once you're clear on the solutions you provide, effective and consistent promotion to your target market will give catapult you over your competitors. Never before have there been such incredible opportunities to promote your business. Unfortunately, along with these, come confusion and a feeling of being overwhelmed.

Why is my medium of choice to write and publish books? Because once you write a book, it lasts forever meaning you can use it over and over in your marketing. Not forgetting, books are also great for getting high fees as a keynote speaker, media coverage, expanding into training programs, using as lead magnets, quality conversion tools and high-quality sales conversations. So much better than a business card!

So how does writing your bestselling book help you achieve freedom? I'll be honest and tell you that very few authors get rich from selling copies of their books. Firstly, it's about being in the right books, and then it's what you do with them to bring in regular, highly-profitable, new and referral business. So, let me walk you through what I call the Celebranding™ model.

Case Study: The Celebrity Experts Celebranding™ Model

Celebranding™ is building your follower base out to thousands of your ideal prospects and clients and positioning yourself as an authority to build trust and shorten your sales cycles.

It is human nature for others to assign "authority" to you when you position yourself to an audience of thousands. Your book allows you to compete against and collaborate with other experts who have spent decades building their credibility and brands.

I'm going to walk you through this system step-by-step. This ensures you understand why we start at the finish with your end goal and how we reverse engineer to grow your business.

First, you need to be clear about your niche, ideal target market and WHAT topic you want to be perceived as an expert on. I encourage my clients to achieve clarity about what they offer and/or which solution to market.

Let's be clear, your offer needs to be the perfect offer. What makes the perfect offer, you ask? Your 'perfect offer' is exactly what your ideal prospect has been looking for.

You want to position yourself with such authority and credibility that the decision for them to hire you, buy your program or product is a no-brainer. It doesn't matter if you offer a one-to-one consulting service or group consulting programs, with this system your target prospects will want to buy it from you much more readily.

The best thing is that your offer is not only perfect for your clients – it's perfect for you. You can charge higher fees, attract more quality clients, and deliver to and service your clients in the best way possible, while still allowing you to scale your business, without ever being overwhelmed.

There are just two simple rules for the perfect offer. First, it must be premium priced. Second, it must leverage your time. We'll look at why raising your prices to a premium price is the difference between success and failure for you. Plus, I'm going to share with you how you can start commanding premium prices even if nobody has ever heard of you before.

Without a leveraged offer, you are merely trading time for money, and this is the most common mistake I see experts make. They trap themselves from the very start – and are unable to grow or scale. Essentially, they're creating a job for themselves and in many cases one that's not very well-paid.

In this case, if you don't put in the hours, you don't get paid. What happens when you want to take a holiday or worse, you get sick like I did? You don't get paid. The money stops coming in. Although this is a common problem that I still see experts facing today, I have, over the years, quietly helped experts overcome this bottleneck.

When you put this system in place, you will discover the ultimate freedom within your consulting business.

The secret to freeing-up your time for your elite clients and projects? Move more of your expertise into a one-to-many environment…

You may have noticed that you end up teaching the same core principles to your new clients, no matter if you're a life coach, a health expert, a business consultant, or whatever. There are core basic principles that every client needs to understand to advance. These principles can be recorded once and then be turned into books and companion training programs.

Topic Ideas for your Books

❯ Plan a book series – this way you can hone in on topics of interest and expertise

❯ 101 Top Tips

❯ 21 Success Strategies

❯ 10 Most Common Mistakes

❯ 1001 Ways to … (this will take a lot longer than 24 hours to complete but done right can become industry textbooks and long-term best sellers!)

Planning Your Book Content

1. What are your top 10-12 teaching points? What are the main points you want to cover in your book?

_____

_____

_____

_____

_____

_____

_____

2. Write out 10 ways you can best help your ideal clients

_____

_____

_____

_____

_____

_____

3. In 1-2 sentences, write out the key message for each of these chapters.

_____

_____

_____

_____

_____

_____

To help, would you like a copy of my step-by-step book planning and launch checklist? We use it when ghostwriting books for our author clients.

Email us at support@celebrityexperts.com and we'll send you the latest version.

CHAPTER 3
STEP 3: Storyboard Your Book

Advertising agencies have been using storyboards for decades to communicate their artistic vision for advertisements. You can use this technique too to map out the story you'll tell your readers.

Start with a whiteboard or big sketchpad, whiteboard pens of different colors, a few different colors of sticky notes (if you think you'll be moving topics and training points around till you get it right).

Bring your book to life by planning it out in the following format:

1. **Chapter topics**

2. **Main points you want to make**

3. **Stories that help your readers understand your points**

4. **Case studies or examples, ideally from your own business**

5. **Invitation to work with you**

Who Doesn't Love a Good Story?

Good news! Once you've outlined your book in this way – the hard work is done. Now, it's just about telling your stories, sharing your wisdom and the experience you've collected over your lifetime.

It becomes more accessible and more pleasurable for a customer to understand and relate to your product through a story. Like all good stories, it needs a start, middle and an end to fully outline your fantastic product or program and the agony points it solves.

You can personalize your narrative by adding stories about your clients' challenges and their ultimate successes.

Your narrative will be an ongoing and organic story that continues for decades.

Start with one color pen or sticky note and put your chapter headings/main topics on your book plan.

Then list each of your supporting topics in another color under the main headings.

When you're satisfied with the overall structure – start writing or dictating in more detail about each of the topics. If you get stuck on a particular topic, leave it and move onto the ones that come more easily.

You can always come back to the ones that need work at the end, and by then you will have had a chance to do some research. Maybe you'll find you don't even need to include these topics. The main thing here is that you do not let these sticking points delay you from completing the bulk of your book.

For example, I was writing a book that explains the system my clients and I use for building our celebrity expert status. I had outlined about 100 topics to cover in the book.

I realized that after two decades in this field that I have enough topics for about 10 books. So, I broke it all up into more manageable topic chunks.

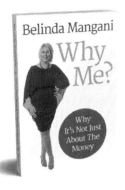

Another example I can give you is of my client Belinda Mangani. She was really stuck trying to fit her story, her money management program and her knowledge of home loans all into one book.

Finally, in a coaching call we discussed breaking it up into three books, and that was all she needed! She quickly completed three complete, complementary books and sells them as a book set to help her clients transform their relationship with money and debt.

If you're finding that you can't make your information work as one book, perhaps it's time to split some of the data into other books in your series?

If you're finding you don't have quite enough to fill one 50-100-page book, but believe you've covered the topic sufficiently, the good news is that many people really appreciate you making the information concise. Don't forget, you can support your text with images and examples.

CHAPTER 4
STEP 4: Dictate or Write Your Book

For some people, the writing part comes easily once they have the structure or outline in place. For others, it helps to 'talk' or dictate the book in a conversational or teaching style.

For most of my clients putting four to five hours aside (with NO distractions) to dictate or write up the bulk of your book will be enough. You'll get the bulk of it written in one day and can spend the next day filling gaps and adding in more value. Then you can hire one of our professional writers to finish it off to a professional level in just a few hours.

Remember, your goal is not to give away every aspect of your knowledge and expertise in your books, but to show your ideal customers that you are qualified in your area of expertise. You want to show enough skill while leaving the concepts open so that potential clients can apply them to their problems.

I find it's easiest if I plan out how I would train a group on the topic and script out that training. This helps me balance out the content, structure it and make sure I don't forget any important details. It also helps to keep the information accessible if you focus on the needs of your reader or potential trainee.

You can write or dictate this part. To dictate there are phone apps, or several online applications available to record your experiences into a document. There are also excellent transcription services, and I know a lot of experts recommend **Rev.com** for transcription, subtitles, captions and all kinds of other cool extras.

Descript.com is also pretty good for transcription if you speak very clearly.

Below you will find lots of questions to get you started and inspire you to come up with great stories and experiences that have inspired you or taught you what you know today.

You will also find a standard outline for your book, so you know how to piece it all together. I've included most of the elements you will want to add to your book, but it's entirely up to you to choose. You might, for example, want to keep it simple, especially if your book is going to be purely digital as a PDF document.

To create your PDF digital book, set your document to the following standards:

Page Size: For Europe, Australia A4 (210mmx297mm), for the US Letter Size (8.5"x11")

Font Size and Line Spacing: Standard legible fonts such as Times New Roman, Arial, Calibri or Verdana 14 point, with 22 size headings, 1.5 or double spacing for easy reading.

Margins: 20mm-25mm wide, (0.78"-0.98"), left, right, top and bottom

Footer: Page numbers, book title – left aligned,

© Your company name, right aligned

A call-to-action clickable link inviting clients to a sales page, offer or to learn more

Make the copy in your footer 75% grey tone so it's lighter than the main body copy color.

Images: All images and diagrams must be copyright free to use, clear and for printing quality at least 300dpi resolution. For a digital only book the images can be lower resolution. For commercial books, we source images from stock photo sites such as **Depositphotos.com** and **Shutterstock.com**. There are some free sites, but check the use of the images are approved to use for commercial purposes, such as books.

Please seek your own legal advice about copyright, trademarks and intellectual property protections.

Sample Template For Your Book

Cover Page – Draft Title, Draft Sub Title, Author

❯ **Copyright and legal page.**

State your copyright and the allowed use of your intellectual property.

Do you need to include any disclaimers such as consult your professional adviser, healthcare provider or earnings associate?

❯ **Summary of the Book Promise**

What are the main outcomes people will achieve from reading your book?

Write up a brief description of the book and focus on the benefits and outcomes for readers

❯ **About the Author** (here's where you connect with your readers and list your relevant accomplishments)

❯ **Bonus offer** to invite readers to join your mailing list or book in for something valuable

❯ **Table of Contents** (if you use our team to professionally design your book we'll create the Table of Contents)

❯ **Dedication, Acknowledgements, Foreword** (all optional)

❯ **Introduction**

❯ **Chapters**

❯ **Conclusion**

❯ **Endorsements** (glowing reviews from clients or peers)

❯ **Bonus Offer** (can be the same as earlier or another offer)

❯ **About your services or programs / other books** (optional)

❯ **Appendix, Index or Definitions** (optional)

Shortcut: Using Content You've Already Compiled or Written

Can you include any copies of any marketing pieces you have already written? These include sales letters, advertisements, brochures, and testimonials from satisfied customers, any articles on your business, marketing plans, etc.

Helpful questions for creating content:

1. What inspired you to get into your field?

_____

_____

_____

_____

2. Were there any turning points in your life that changed everything?

_____

_____

_____

_____

3. What have you learned from your failures in life?

_____

_____

_____

_____

4. What have you learned from your successes in life?

_____

_____

_____

_____

5. What have you learned from mentors in your life?

_____

_____

_____

_____

6. What are the most common mistakes you see people making that you can help with?

_____

_____

_____

_____

7. Do you have any services or systems that are transformational?

_____

_____

_____

_____

8. Share some stories about people or companies you've helped and how

_____

_____

_____

_____

9. What outcomes can you guarantee or at least strive for?

_____

_____

_____

_____

10. How can people work with you?

_____

_____

_____

_____

Adding Motivational Quotes

Are there any notable quotes or sayings which you live your life by?

You can find lots of famous quotes online. Including them in your book can add value. Just make sure you get the quotes right and that you attribute them to author.

Another way to add value to your book is to include impressive statistics, short stories, examples or case studies.

Adding Case Studies

Case Studies can be hugely influential and a way of showing off the fantastic outcomes you achieve for your clients while being high-value learning experiences for your readers at the same time.

Consider placing case studies throughout your book, or all together as a section at the beginning or end of your book.

Writing Your 'About the Author' Bio

At the start or end of your book, you should tell the readers about you. After all, this is a book to showcase you as a solutions provider. So, don't miss the opportunity to tell them all about you.

I don't mean to alarm you, but your professional bio can affect your sales, your conversion rates, how often you're paid to speak at events, how attractive you are to the media, and how eagerly people will line up to work with or hire you. Because it will be posted in so many more places, your bio can have more impact than what you write in your book!

Keep your bio short, concise and interesting.

This is your chance! Tell us about you.

This should give us some background about you as the author and how you became interested and experienced in this topic.

_____

_____

_____

_____

Is there anything about you or your business that will lend credibility to your book and business? This might include any awards you have won, how long you have been in business, your clients, how many people you've helped before, the number of locations you have. List your achievements, impressive clients, books you've written, your main websites, and how to connect with you on social media.

_____

_____

_____

_____

List interesting/exciting things you've done in your life, and/or that you want to do. Is there anything else interesting about you, like living with unusual pets, fostering children, or helping charities? What are your hobbies and passions?

_____

_____

_____

_____

_____

_____

List any programs that you offer/plan to offer

_____

_____

_____

Review Your Professional Bio Regularly

It's worth reviewing your professional and author biography on a regular basis. For instance, now that you're in the process of writing a book you can add author to your bio. Make sure your bio very clearly showcases who you help, what ideal clients hire you and for what outcomes, and ways that your ideal clients can work with you.

Remember to regularly read and, if necessary, update your Linkedin bio and any website bios regularly too. Other professionals and potential clients will Google you, so make sure you're one step ahead and making the best impression. Simply Google yourself and see what results come up. You can then review these and update where necessary.

My Amazon Author Profile

Cydney O'Sullivan

✓ Following

Cydney O'Sullivan is an enthusiastic entrepreneur, author and publisher. She is a caring mentor with 30 years experience building businesses through her training programs 'BestSellerSuccess.com' and

Author Updates

This is how I appear on Page 1 of Google when I search for my name. See how the books show up?

CHAPTER 5
STEP 5: Edit & Review Your Book

Do not skip this step. One of the most damaging things you can do is to write your book and NOT have a professional proofreader check through it. Your book needs to represent you in the best and most flattering way. A book that is full of typo's, poor spelling, grammar and other mistakes will make you appear unprofessional to prospects and peers.

Firstly, decide which language to set your document to for spell check purposes. Is your book primarily for Australian or UK customers? Or for the wider US market? US readers generally prefer US spellings, and as a smaller population, Australians are usually tolerant of US spellings.

Run the spell checker through Word (or whatever system you're using), remembering that this isn't going to catch every error. It will, however, help you pick up some of the things you have missed.

Read through, review and go through the document at least a few times until you're happy with it. Then send it to a professional proofreader, editor, and while you're at it, any friends who are passionate readers or interested in your topic. You'll be surprised at the mistakes your friends will find that both you and the editor missed!

I'm not suggesting that your editor or your friends should completely rewrite your book – this is a common problem with some editors (and friends), it's your book, so be open to feedback, but firm in your convictions.

For printed books the publishing standard is to start all chapters on the right hand side of the book, so you may end up with some blank pages.

Bonus Success Tip:

If you're going to get some friends and peers to review your book, why not ask them to provide endorsements at the same time?

Who can you ask for endorsements or testimonials?

If you're new to collecting testimonials and endorsements, this is a great way to start. Draft a selection of (truthful) sample endorsements for your book. Creating a guide to what to write makes it easier for your reviewers. Most of your clients and peers will be delighted that you've asked them to read your book and happy to provide a testimonial or review.

CHAPTER 6
STEP 6: Format Your Book and Cover

If you're planning to distribute your book in PDF format (as a digital document), you can format it using a word processing system and make sure that it looks neat, organized and professional.

Make sure you include all your regular links so that readers can connect with you via your book. Ideally, these will be in the footer or header.

Include page numbers, your book title and your name as the author on every other page at least.

We like to go the extra mile and format our client's books for printing as paperbacks, for publishing on Kindle or other platforms such as iTunes and as PDF digital books. As publishers we have talented book designers on our team, so we want our own and our client's books to look as appealing as possible.

> **Take extra care with your book cover. Despite what you have heard, people really do judge a book by its cover.**

Some Things To Keep in Mind for Your Book Cover

1. Many books today will be viewed on a phone, tablet, eReader or other small devices so keep your title and subtitle large and clear for ease of reading.

2. Take time choosing the right images for your cover. Publishing standards require images to be at least 300dpi resolution for printing quality. You do not want any fuzzy or grainy images anywhere on your book. If you're only distributing your books digitally, you can use lower resolution images like the ones you use on your websites and social media.

3. Remember your brand colors and fonts – try to keep consistent with your branding on your book covers too.

4. Make sure you aren't violating anyone else's copyright or trademarks. Many images you'll see online are owned by the creator or photographer, so you can't just borrow them without permission. To find out more about intellectual property laws, there's an excellent chapter on the topic in my book Social Marketing Superstars. You can also consult with a legal adviser or do more of your own research.

5. Take some time to look at other books in your genre or about your topic. Look in bookshops or online book marketplaces. Get a feel for the kind of cover designs the top ranking, best-selling authors are using for their books. If in doubt about how to design your book cover, err on the side of caution. It's better to keep your front cover elegant and straightforward.

Examples of Best Selling Business Book Cover Designs on <u>Amazon.com</u> at time of writing – do you notice a theme?

Notice how most of them have strong, short titles, minimal images and plain covers.

White covers look beautiful in the bookstore but can fail to 'pop' on-line against white backgrounds. Notice, however, how the yellow covers stand out?

Consider How Your Book Will Be Working For YOU!

Examples of some book covers we designed for clients – whose books are strategically written and designed for enhancing 'Celebrity Expert' authority status.

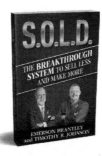
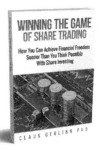

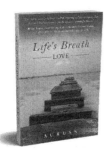

CHAPTER 7
STEP 7: Share Your Book

Given that this book is about how to Write Your Book FAST from here on you will find lots of bonus advice to inspire and assist you to achieve greater success!

Once your book has been written, proofed and edited, I suggest promoting it to a group of your target market to test it. Ask for their honest feedback. This is an opportunity not only to have fun but to collect some very valuable market research. You can also ask them to share their top tips, their most significant challenges, to reveal the biggest problem in their business and in their lives, etc. Consider offering them a nice reward, such as another useful tool, resource or some of your time if you can spare it. This is an excellent way of getting to know the genuine challenges of your target market.

You can implement all the useful feedback into your book and begin working on the emails and sales pages to support the release. If you're publishing to online platforms such as Amazon or iBooks, you'll need a book description that compels readers to buy your book. If on the other hand, you're promoting the book directly to your audiences and followers, you will need emails and compelling copy explaining all the reasons why they need your book right now!

If you are selling or giving away the book yourself, you can set up a professional sales page and payment processing. Be sure to test that the sales pages function correctly.

When you're ready to release your book to the public, think about doing a big launch – with emails, social media and ad campaigns.

Consider your book as a valuable means of adding new customers and targeted prospects to your database. Remember that your book purchasers are highly qualified and interested in your topic. More so than those who pick it up as a free book offer.

Experienced marketers will tell you that "a buyer is a buyer is a buyer", and that anyone who becomes a 'buyer of your information' is much more likely to continue to invest in your solutions and programs **if** you continue to effectively communicate and provide valuable solutions to your target market.

CONCLUSION

Now Go Write Your Book!

If you haven't been writing your book while reading through this one, then I encourage you to go do so right now! I wrote most of this book in 1 day, and over the next couple of days added in all the bonus content.

The worst part is finding the discipline to plan for 2-3 hours, but once you've done that, then you just have to find the discipline to spend another 2-3 hours on your content, and then another, and before you know it your book will be all done!

You can do this! You know your topic.

If you still feel unsure or confused, or just aren't finding the time – contact us, we're here to help.

What's Next? I hope you've enjoyed and received lots of value from this book... if you have consider joining our author coaching program at

www.CelebrityBlueprint.com

You'll have access to ongoing trainings on writing your books to marketing your books and business, and a supportive author community to share your journey with!

I hope to hear from you.

In the meantime please recommend this book to anyone you know who wants to write their book!

Please direct them to our sales page, we need the revenue from the sales of the book to pay for the marketing to help more people achieve success and live their dreams!

Thank you and to your great success!

BONUS CHAPTER 1
Get Published – Get Noticed!

First off, finish your book...

So, you still think you've got a book in you? Great. Start and finish it! Remember, your book will showcase your expertise in your field and solve agony points aplenty. Completing your book does not have to be costly, even if you use a ghostwriter.

Consider the opportunities and time lost if you don't get it finished. You need to be prepared to commit to this project as you want to do a good job. It's something you will put your name to and feel proud of after all.

 Along with the main body of work, your completed book will now include a combination of endorsements, legals, a dedication, author bio, TOC, foreword, intro, chapters, epilogue/conclusion, resources and an index.

To create a professional finish (and before you present it for potential publication), you will need to have your book edited and proofed. Use our team at **www.CelebrityExperts.com**, ask for recommendations from other authors or search online to find professional editors and designers.

If your goal is to publish your book in as many places as possible, you will need to format it for all the different publishing platforms. We can help you to format and publish on the major platforms such as Amazon, Kindle and Ingram/Lightning Source and Smashwords.

Finding a Literary Agent

If you're looking for a publishing contract with one of the major international publishers, you will need a literary agent. Agents specialize in genres, subject and styles of writing, so it's a waste of your time (and theirs) if you target every agent you find. It doesn't take much research to see which agents specialise in your field.

We have relationships with many of the big international publishers and literary agents and can help you prepare your book proposals as one of our services. However, most of our clients usually choose to self-publish or have us publish on their behalf as we are very fast to market.

We recently published a client's book from manuscript to overnight shipping in just 7 days, because they needed it for their event.

Getting a publishing contract with a larger publisher generally takes months, sometimes years, and then it can still take months or years on top of that to get the book out into the market. Sadly, many books published by the larger publishers are unsuccessful.

This causes other problems such as having to pay hefty fees or being asked to buy back your book. Always get professional advice and read through the publishing contract.

If you still want to explore the route of a finding an agent, create a list of all the relevant agents and then dig a little deeper, to find feedback or reviews. After you've done this, you can split the agents into groups, with your favored agents at the top.

 By the way, it's okay to contact more than one agent at a time. In fact, you'll be buffering the likely rejections you'll receive as well as using your time wisely.

Contacting Agents On Your Hit List

So, you've created a list of agents that are a good match for your book. Next, you must write a letter that will include, amongst other things, a proposal outlining details about yourself and your background. You can then explain what the book is about and why you've written it.

Your proposal can chart the content of your book from start to finish, but you still need to tell the agent *why* you are the right person to write it. Your book could well be 'niche' so you can't expect every agent to understand or have even heard about the subject area. You need to make it clear why this book needs to be read and by whom.

It's your agent's job to sell your book to a publisher, but you need to make the reasons why they should sell it easy enough to understand. They need to grasp what it is that you're trying to achieve and work out how and to whom they can sell it.

Likely outcomes of contacting an agent are that they either send a polite rejection or they ask to see an example chapter or two. The agent's website will most probably include details outlining the format and whether they like to receive sample chapters. Do yourself a favor – do your homework before making contact.

Your letter is your opening gambit and possibly your 'make or break' interaction with an agent. It, therefore, pays to put in the effort and pitch it correctly. You are selling your product, so don't be afraid to make it clear why your book is needed (with research to back you up) and how it is different to anything else on the market.

After you've submitted your letter and proposal, it could be some time before you get a response (if any). Try not to feel too downhearted if you get rejections from agents; this is the norm in a very competitive industry. In fact, it may be a long time until you get a positive outcome.

In the meantime, it's imperative that you keep plugging away and messaging agents working your way down your list. It can sometimes help if you give yourself a realistic timeline such as one year. If, after this time, you are still no further forward in your search perhaps it's time to re-examine your letter and your approach. Maybe it needs to be re-worded?

Deciding Which Agent

If you're in the fortunate position of having interest from more than one agent, you'll need to determine which one is the right fit for you. It can sometimes come down to what they can offer you and just the simple fact that you like them! The latter, by the way, shouldn't be overlooked as you could be working with them for a long time and on a very regular basis.

What Does An Agent Do?

An agent knows the market and what's in demand. Don't be surprised if they give you feedback in the shape of edits and amendments before they even consider showing your book to publishers. Often this could mean deleting what you believe to be some of your best work. My advice? Take it on the chin unless it doesn't feel right. In which case, you are entitled to stand your ground and fight for a paragraph/chapter that you think is justified.

It's only when, and if, your agent thinks that your book is in the right shape that they will take it out to publishers. Just like you had to wait to find the right agent, you can expect to wait a long time until you hear back from any publishers. It's your agent's job to keep on top of contacting publishers. They'll let you know when they have feedback or, fingers crossed, some good news!

BONUS CHAPTER 2
Choosing Your Publisher

You are to be congratulated if you get to a stage where you are choosing between publishers. Whereas there's little to negotiate between selecting agents there *are* things to consider when picking your publisher.

Your agent is ultimately responsible for the chief negotiations, but you still need to be in the loop. Make sure you understand what each publisher brings to the table such as payment times (up front, installments or post-publishing) or percentage of sales. As with choosing your agent, a good relationship with your publisher is essential – you could be together for the long haul.

If you'd rather focus on getting your book to market fast and efficiently, consider a boutique publisher like our services at **CelebrityExperts.com**. We generally look for ways to share the costs of professionally publishing and promoting a client's book. We do this with an eye to a long-term relationship where we build your celebrity expert status through marketing and promotion. You can find out more about our services on our website.

Working With Your Publisher

Just as your agent will ask for edits and amends, your publisher is likely to do the same. As they know the market well, you should listen to their views and then weigh them up. If you feel strongly that your Chapter 3 needs to stay, then you are within your rights to voice your concerns – but do so with a certain degree of flexibility thrown in.

Sometimes projects falter. Disagreements may happen (but are rare) or staff move on and your book gets put to one side. Don't lose heart. If your book raised interest before, it is likely to do so again. Your agent will hopefully find another publisher.

Pre-Publication

If your book is on its way to publication, it doesn't mean you can rest on your laurels. Instead, you should be out there drumming up interest. For example, take to your social media and build your followers. Make sure you post regularly to create hype. There's no doubt you'll be excited about your book but try to get your followers excited too. That way, by publication day they'll be chomping at the bit to get hold of a copy.

Reviews on book sites such as **Amazon.com** are important but getting approval from them can be very challenging. Getting a group of supporters on-board to post genuine reviews for your book on release day can really help.

Your publisher can also arrange an advertising schedule to promote your book pre-sale.

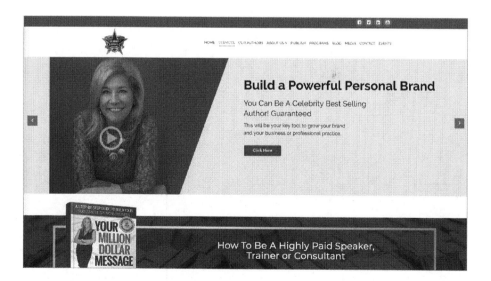

BONUS CHAPTER 3
Published? Get Selling!

Imagine how it feels to hold your published book in all its glory. Or to have your book set up as part of an automated marketing campaign generating hundreds to thousands of targeted leads for your business.

What a journey! But this is not the end. To make the most of your book continue plugging away on social media, interacting with your followers and seeking out opportunities to promote your book. Signings, appearances on radio or TV, guest blogs and posts, podcasts, articles – you name it. Do them.

Other Revenue Generating Ideas
Give Your Book Wings

You've written a book. Now what? Knowing what to do and where to take your book is essential. Far more than the constraints of its binding, your book can lead your readers to your other revenue generating streams. In this chapter, I've condensed the most important lessons I've learned in my 15+ year career as a 16 times best-selling author. Here goes…

Let Them Hear Your Voice…

Listen up. Audiobooks are big news, so big in fact that last year, in the US alone, they made around 2.5 billion dollars in sales and are the fastest growing sector in digital publishing. If you haven't already, now's the time to adapt your book to audio.

(**https://goodereader.com/blog/audiobooks/global-audiobook-trends-and-statistics-for-2018**)

What makes audiobooks so popular? Reading a book takes a fair bit of effort but listening to one is effortless. Face it, how easy is it to press the play arrow on our smartphones and listen to an audiobook AND do something else (drive, cook, close your eyes) at the same time?

Research the options available to you regarding your budget, location and requirements. Either download the software and create your own audiobook or (depending on your budget), employ a professional to do it for you.

Let Them Hear and See You...

Go one step further and take your book on the road. Appearing at seminars gives you a chance to engage with a large group of people. Enthral, entertain and teach them a few of the best tricks you've learned along the way, not forgetting to let them know about your must-have products and services. Never doubt the fact that opportunities to appear as a keynote speaker add kudos and valuable credentials to your resume.

These opportunities are a two-way street – the audience learns from the expertise you've accrued over the years. In return, you build up your contacts and get to network with a captured audience who will take up your services and possibly buy your book (if they haven't already).

Take To The Virtual Stage

If the thought of touring the country (or countries) and appearing in front of audiences is not for you, consider the internet as your conference medium. With the growing sophistication and set-up of virtual classrooms and video messaging you can host conferences, consultations, coaching sessions, mentoring groups or one-on-one case studies from your home/office. The virtual world is your oyster.

The cost of your virtual services will vary depending on the number of sessions, participants involved, and time taken. For example, if you are a life coach, you might offer a coaching session on 'Learning to Set Boundaries.' You'll promote this to your contacts group and feature it on your social media. You will charge a one-off fee for a 60-minute training session via video link. To extend this, you will then offer one-to-one consultations for those who want extra help or advice.

Tap Into The eBook Gold Rush

Who doesn't love their e-reader? It makes absolute sense to have your book available in this format. Far from difficult, you can adapt your book to the eBook market and make it accessible to the various platforms. As an eBook, your tome delivers extra services. Not only is it a good read, but it›s also more transportable and serves as a searchable, reference guide and brilliant lead magnet or sales conversion magnifier.

Within your eBook, you can include working links to your website, services, social media as well as sites/blogs or posts that are relevant.

Finally, an enticing factor worth remembering about eBooks is that when you sell the book online, your only cost is the setup and delivery of a digital file. Even on the publishing platforms royalties can be generous.

Hook Up With Other Like-Minded Individuals

Collaboration creates value for you and your target customers. If you can, find other experts in your business sector who are also looking to lead readers.

As a dog trainer you could, for example, group together with a start-up pet food company, an animal hotel and a vet. Together, you will create a package of eBooks/conferences/virtual conferences or consultancy packages and market theses to a combined contacts list.

Turn Your Book Into A Course

Don›t be surprised to discover that a lot of readers will want to dig deeper into your insight and knowledge. A course, therefore, is the perfect vehicle. Online courses are a very popular means of sharing expertise. The structure of your course can follow the chapters in your book (or not). Many online courses include video commentary and a combination of workbooks, journaling, quizzes and case studies. You can create interactive exercises as well as the more ordinary pen to paper ones to generate something that will excite the student.

As for extras, you can include any audio clips, videos, PDFs and demonstrations that you have and/or create new ones. Many courses have Facebook groups where students can interact and ask questions.

Join our author community Facebook Group: Celebrity Book Club

> Get notice of free and 99c books we're launching

> Get advice and tips to sell more books

https://www.facebook.com/groups/celebrityexperts/

Taking it one step further, consider giving accreditation and/or certification on completion of your course. With training, these customers can take your knowledge and teach others 'your way'. The amount of influence in being the name behind a training method is immense.

Adding Value To Your Existing Book

What if I was to say you only need to do one thing to your current book to generate more impact? It sounds simple but 'pimping up' your current book by adding a hardcover can be very effective. Why? A hardcover smacks of luxury and expense and rightly so.

Hardcovers can be pricey, but with a bit of savvy shopping and negotiation, it's possible to buy bulk and get a decent discount. Your hardcover book(s) will make great presents, competition prizes or a 'gift' at a seminar or meeting.

I hope you can see that there are no limits as to where your book can go. If you want to use your book to lead readers on a journey, all you need to do is give it wings…

BONUS CHAPTER 4
How To Publicize Your Book

You've worked like crazy to produce a book that you are proud of. Now, you want to make sure that it is bought and read. To do this, you need to publicize.

There are plenty of ways to contact the media to get coverage for your book, and, contrary to belief, most of them will require you to do the donkey work. Be prepared to come up with feature ideas, suggestions, to put together facts and figures and arrange meetings. And, after all that, a journalist may decide that YOU are as much of a story as your book. Or not.

What Does Your Ideal Customer Read/Watch/Listen To?

If your niche product is in the pet's arena, it's unlikely that Indoor Plants Monthly magazine will be interested in your book. Knuckle down and research all the relevant media outlets. Also consider what other media your ideal customer reads – as in women's magazine, men's magazines, local and national papers and what radio and TV they tune into.

Prepare A Winning Press Release

Put together a professional press release. If you're unsure how to do this try searching online for examples from big organizations.

In a nutshell, press releases are no more than a few hundred words, contain only information that is newsworthy (the more flowery parts can be added to the story by the journalist), have all dates and contacts and if relevant, links to pictures. If you have space, include bullet-pointed ideas with feature ideas.

What Is Your Book's USP?

There's something different about your book, isn't there? You know it, but that media outlet doesn't. Wherever possible, try to highlight the unique aspects of your book. This will include mentioning notable things about you, your work history, your family life or the like. Don't be shy – stand out from the crowd.

Keep Abreast Of The News

It pays to follow the news like a hawk and be ready to pounce on any stories related to your book. If you've written a book about losing weight and new research comes out saying that the population is more over-weight than it was ten years ago – jump on it and save people the task of finding an expert. Start contacting media and offering yourself up for interviews, blogs, articles and anything else that you can do to promote your book.

If you are unable to regularly monitor news, think about subscribing to news alerts. You can input keywords, and when anything related to these crops up in reports, you are notified.

The Story Could Be You

How do you feel about being in the public eye? A journalist might think that you are more of a story than your book, especially when it comes to Non-Fiction. So, get your own life story in order and be prepared to face some questioning. As daunting as this sounds, many people find this part of the media process a lot of fun, especially if you enjoy meeting and talking with new contacts.

Keep Your Pitch Perfect

No doubt you have thousands of things you can tell the media about your book. Be that as it may, it's far better to keep any pitch short and to the point rather than overload (and possibly bore) with pages and pages of information.

If you can lure in some media interest, there will be time to expand later.

As mentioned before, a pitch can be tied into:

❯ Newsworthy events

❯ Dates

❯ Seasonal (e.g. Valentine's Day, Christmas, Easter)

❯ Trending opinions/actions

❯ Viral activity

Some Basic Do's And Don'ts

❯ DO Pitch to one person only in each organization

❯ DO Follow up emails with another email suggesting a slightly different angle

❯ DO Ditch paper press kits – think of the trees (do it online)

❯ DON'T nag or hassle – you will get nowhere by being annoying

❯ DON'T forget grammar, spelling and to check names and places

❯ DO create your own media suite on your site with links to information, pictures and other facts and figures.

❯ DO keep on top of your social media – it provides invaluable insight into current conversations and trends.

10 Top Tips For Guest Blogging to Become A Celebrity Expert

If you're an Author or Speaker, be aware of the importance of personal branding. The reputation that you build for yourself is one of your most valuable assets, and it's what helps you to increase your speaking fees and get bigger crowds when booked for engagements.

Blogging can be a great way to establish thought-leadership, celebrity and to build your online brand. If you're not getting the results you'd like, the chances are that you've got your strategy wrong.

Guest blogging on reputable sites is a great way to drive targeted traffic back to your website, and you might find that reaching out to these sites and offering to contribute is a better use of your time than writing on your own website. This is especially true if you specialize in a industry. For example, if you make a living in the travel industry, reaching out to Travel Industry sites makes more sense than posting on Facebook, even though it has a smaller readership

Here are some tips for success when reaching out to Publications as a celebrity expert.

1. **Write the post beforehand**

    Some publishers will want to see your whole post instead of just receiving a pitch. If you're serious about your blogger outreach campaign, then it's a good idea to write your posts beforehand to save time, then if nobody else wants to publish it, you can always use it on your own site.

2. **Proofread and edit**

    This applies to everything from your pitch email and the subsequent communications to the blog post itself. Always read back through it and make any tweaks that are needed to improve the flow or to correct the spelling and grammar. If you want people to take you seriously as an expert, it's important to appear professional at all times – and nothing makes you look more unprofessional than a spelling mistake.

3. **Listen to feedback**

    If a publisher rejects your post and provides a reason for it, learn from that feedback and be prepared to make any changes that they suggest. This is a regular part of the publishing process, and you shouldn't feel disheartened. If you're asked to make changes, be willing to make them – after all, the goal is to make your post the best it can possibly be.

4. **Follow up on your submissions**

The biggest publishers receive dozens if not hundreds of pitches and submissions every day, which means your message can easily get lost or overlooked. Give publishers space after you email them because they are likely to be busy. If you don't hear back from them after a week or two, drop them a message to see what's up.

5. **Specialize in a certain industry**

If you choose to specialize in a specific sector, you'll be able to build up a more established reputation. Once you've written for one publication, you'll find it easier to be accepted by others. On top of that, finding a niche will help your career in general because it makes it easier to rise to the top and to command a premium.

6. **Read!**

Don't just blindly approach different blog sites. Take a little time to read their recent articles and to study the kind of stuff that they're into. Take notes on how long their articles are and what topics are the most popular. This will help you to tailor your approach when you're pitching.

7. **Research publishers' style**

Different publishers have different styles, and if you don't know what I mean then compare Buzzfeed to The New York Times. You'll see that some are clickbaity and conversational while others are in-depth or analytical. Many publishers have their own style guidelines when it comes to the way that they write, so be sure to check before you pitch to them.

8. **Join the community**

    Many publishers, and particularly those who specialize in a specific niche, have successfully built a community around themselves, whether it's on social networking sites or right there in the comments section of their website. The good news is that you can join this community by leaving comments on recent posts and taking the time to chat with other readers.

9. **Obey submission guidelines**

    Publishers that accept guest posts aim to make it as easy as possible for you to take part by providing submission guidelines. These guidelines usually describe precisely what they're looking for. This means you can ensure that your pitch and post both adhere to the given instructions. If your submission doesn't subscribe to guidelines, they're much less likely to accept it.

10. **What's Next?**

    Guest blogging is just one of many ways to get the word out there and to establish your personal brand. But at the same time, as a public speaker, it's understandable if you'd prefer to use your voice instead of writing a blog post.

10 Top Tips To Get Featured on Podcasts as a Celebrity Expert

Podcasts are often overlooked as a marketing tool, but the truth is that they're an underutilized utility and therefore easier to cut through the noise. Approximately nine million Americans listen to six or more podcasts every week, while over a quarter of American men have listened to a podcast in the last month.

In fact, podcasting can be a fantastic way to expand your reach while simultaneously branding yourself as an authority in your niche. Here are my top tips to boost your public speaking business by appearing on a podcast.

1. **Find your niche**

    In the same way that it's a good idea to specialize in a niche when launching a blogger outreach campaign, it's a good idea to narrow down in your search for podcasts. The more relevant the podcast is to what you do, the more likely they are to respond positively when you pitch to them.

2. **Check directories**

    Take some time to look in the different podcast directories on services like iTunes to get a good feel for what's on the market. The good thing about these directories is that they also allow you to look at specific genres, which is going to come in handy when you're trying to find your niche.

3. **Get to know the landscape**

    When you're first getting into podcasting, it makes sense to research the most popular podcasts in a variety of different niches to get a feel for what works and what doesn't. This will make it easier for you to judge quality when you approach a podcast and to make sure that you don't waste your time teaming up with someone who'll reflect poorly on your brand.

4. **Look for crossovers**

    While you're researching these popular podcasts, you might find niches that are similar to but not exactly the same as your field of expertise. For example, if you teach people how to become better writers, you might be able to team up with a marketing podcast to share blogging tips or a literary podcast to weigh in on different writing styles.

5. **Listen to the podcast**

   You'd be amazed at how many people fail to listen to the podcasts that they're pitching to. If you don't listen to their show, how can you personalise the message you send? This is vital if you want to catch their attention. Remember, many podcasts receive hundreds or thousands of emails, so you'll need to make sure that you offer something super relevant if you want to pique their interest.

6. **Befriend the host**

   One way to make sure that your pitch isn't ignored is to reach out to the host on social media sites and to join discussions around the show. Make sure that you're contributing to a discussion rather than spamming them! By taking part in the community, you get a chance to demonstrate your expertise while increasing the odds that they recognize your name when it appears in their inbox.

7. **Be clear in your message**

   When you send your email asking for a guest spot, make sure that you ask. Be very clear about what you will contribute and why you want to take part and be sure to include contact details and further links so that they can find out more about you. If you've got a media kit, some press coverage or further proof of your credentials, make sure to share.

8. **Know how it fits in with your marketing plan**

   There's no point appearing on a podcast if it doesn't offer you any value. That's why you'll need to take some time to figure out how you can make the most out of your podcast appearance. Is it by publishing website content about it? Or creating a dedicated landing page for podcast listeners offering a free gift in exchange for their contact information? If you do create a landing page, make sure that the URL is easy to say and remember so that there's no miscommunication when it's time to plug it.

9. **Thank the host**

    After your appearance on the podcast, be sure to drop the host and their team an email to say thanks and to follow up. A good relationship could mean another invitation in the future or allow you to recommend a friend/peer who would like to feature. Stay in touch with the host as time goes by and if there are further developments in the area you discussed, let them know and offer to come back.

10. **Engage on social media**

    If the host has gone out of his/her way to feature you, the least you can do is share the podcast's links on your social networking sites. It's also a good idea to monitor any chatter about the show and to join in with any conversations. This allows you to maintain engagement long after the episode airs.

What's Next?

I hope you've enjoyed and received lots of value from this book... if you have consider joining our author coaching program at

www.CelebrityBlueprint.com

You'll have access to over 50 hours of trainings on writing your books to marketing your books and business, and a supportive author community to share your journey with!

I hope to hear from you.

In the meantime please recommend this book to anyone you know who wants to write their book!

Please direct them to our sales page, we need the revenue from the sales of the book to pay for the marketing to help more people achieve success and live their dreams!

Thank you and to your great success!

RAVING FANS

When I saw the title, even before reading the book, my reaction was: Wow! Who else could have done it if not Cydney?! She truly is the most innovative, inspirational and adventurous writer, speaker and promoter with no comparison around.

In my personal experience, Cydney has helped me so much with creating, editing and making my book possible to come out and being published and getting my Bestseller #1 on Amazon in one month since being released.

I am 78 years old, a health and wellness professional sharing my knowledge and ample scope of experience in my book "The Lukin Longevity System".

However, to convert that knowledge and practice into a book would not have been possible without Cydney and her team.

This is my chance to say Thank you to them one more time. Congratulations on another great book Cydney, and I am sure many more will follow.

Natasha Lukin,
#1 Best Selling Author
The Lukin Longevity System

I have known Cydney for a few years and in that time I have found her to be a woman of true integrity, who is ready to do everything humanly possible to make your book a success. She works long and hard on your success.

She even has more faith in others than many have in themselves. If others in the market place could be as honest and true as Cydney, the world would be a better place to live. I am blessed to be a part of her wide client base. Thank you Cydney."

Carole Stokes, Gold Coast, Queensland, Australia
Author and Speaker

I needed to write to put words to my feelings and feelings into my words. Words are powerful energy and have become imprints on my mind.

It's been an amazing process.

John Gold,
Author Life's Breath - Love

I strongly recommend working with Cydney and her creative team for it has truly transformed my life. Working with Cydney brought me closer to achieving my purpose via my book and program more than anything ever could in my life. What took me 3 years to get started on my own was done with total ease within a few short months with Cydney's team. I am

truly grateful to have the guidance and done for you approach from her team which allows me to focus on giving my best to the world.

If you have a message to give the world then I strongly recommend her team of professionals to help you manifest your dream. I am eternally grateful for working with them, they have transformed my life and helped me transform the lives of many others." I hope you like that as it comes straight from my heart. My life is different today thanks to you and your team. Much blessings!

Dr Stephanie Kabonga,
Author & Motivational Speaker

The writing is the easy part of every book; It's the marketing that can be a proverbial minefield! I am grateful to Cydney for taking me by the hand and making the marketing of my book a walk in the park. Giving me the confidence that I needed, she has helped me to work with my strengths and opened up a world of possibilities for me. Thank you, Cydney! I'd recommend you to any budding author.

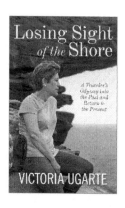

Victoria Ugarte Travel Writer,
Corporate Culture Specialist & Best Selling Author

http://ExploreMyWorldTravel.com

Working with Cydney has been a joy. Her encouragement, enthusiasm and expertise in business consulting, has seen my business take a quantum leap!

Bernie Griffiths,
Director ASWPP Photographer, Author,
Business Strategist Speaker

http://BernieGriffiths.com

I am in the final stages of having my first book published with Cydney O'Sullivan and the Celebrity Experts Team, and am pleased to report the process has been seamless and well above my initial expectations!

As a complete novice in the publishing world, I was very fortunate to have the support, expertise and guidance of Cydney and her talented team members.

If you have a 'story to tell', Cydney has the ability to turn your dreams into a reality!

Julie George,
Author of Million Dollar Host

When embarking on the journey of writing my first book, I knew nothing about the process. Fortunately, a friend recommended Cydney O'Sullivan to me. I have found the prospect of writing & publishing my book extraordinarily daunting.

Obviously the actual writing, the hardest part, was something only I could do. However, there is so much more to getting from that draft manuscript to holding a published book in your hands.

I know there is a vast team of hard working dedicated staff employed by Cydney and the team helped me overcome many of the final hurdles to bring my autobiography "Beware of Friendly Danger" from thin air into reality within less than five weeks.

Cydney has delivered everything she promised efficiently and promptly. She took care of all facets of the publishing process including providing a very capable editor, help with cover design, and advice on photograph inclusion, as well as the final printing.

Most amazingly Cydney organised my first book release in Los Angeles, California, in March 2018 where I proudly celebrated the release of my book at the Celebrate Fast Track event and was a honoured guest at the A - List celebrity Oscar viewing party hosted by Sir Elton John and David Furnish.

Even my readers have commented on the great quality of the book. I have no hesitation in recommending Cydney to any writer wanting to turn their book into reality. Thanks Cydney and your dedicated team who has got me on Bestseller #1 on Amazon in just a few months since the release of my book.

Günther Frantz,
#1 Best Selling Author, Motivational Speaker

Cydney O'sullivan is such a professional in the book writing space and her layers of knowledge and her desire to see you achieve makes her an outstanding individual. It's people like this that are rare but when you find them you realize they are just GOLD!

Thank you Cydney for helping me write my first book! You're an inspiration.

Cath Slatyer,
Author

Thank you for investing in

AUTHOR-IZE

The Speed Authoring System to Grow Your Business FAST

How To Position Yourself As An Authority, Attract Quality Leads, Increase Your Income and Build Your Brand … Effortlessly

Join and receive bonus resources and tools worth over $1,200!

www.CelebrityExperts.com/book-bonuses

Join our email community and each month you'll receive surprise bonuses from the author and contributors worth over $1,200 in value! Please visit the website for more information

Join our free author community on Facebook, you'll be regularly invited to our trainings and tips for authors. I hope you'll join us over at

https://www.facebook.com/groups/celebrityexperts/

Made in the USA
San Bernardino, CA
13 January 2019